DESIGN & DRAW
50 CAT OUTFITS

Illustrated by Christine Sheldon
Text by Elizabeth Golding
Designed by Anton Poitier and Becca Wildman

About This Book

There are 50 cats and kittens to dress in this book! Each of them has a job or hobby to give you a clue about what they might wear. Use colored pencils or felt-tip pens to fill in the missing parts with fabulous fashion. If you need inspiration, there are lots of ideas at the end of the book.

Have fun!

Add some little extras, such as a necklace or striped socks!

Copyright © 2021 iSeek Ltd.

ISBN: 978-1-64722-311-3

This book was conceived, created, and produced by iSeek Ltd. an imprint of Insight Editions

www.insighteditions.com

Insight Editions PO Box 3088 San Rafael, CA 94912

Printed in China

10 9 8 7 6 5 4 3 2 1

I'm a gymnast!

I'm a chef!

I'd like a dress and red bow, please!

I like shopping!

I'm a zookeeper!

I ride horses!

I like to go fishing!

I play soccer!

I'm an Arctic explorer!

I work in a library!

I'm a gardener!

We are nurses!

Dress me up as a monster!

I am a firefighter!

I like running!

I like to jump!

I like cooking!

Make me a queen!

Make me a king!

I'm a vet!

We like to go swimming!

I'm a carpenter!

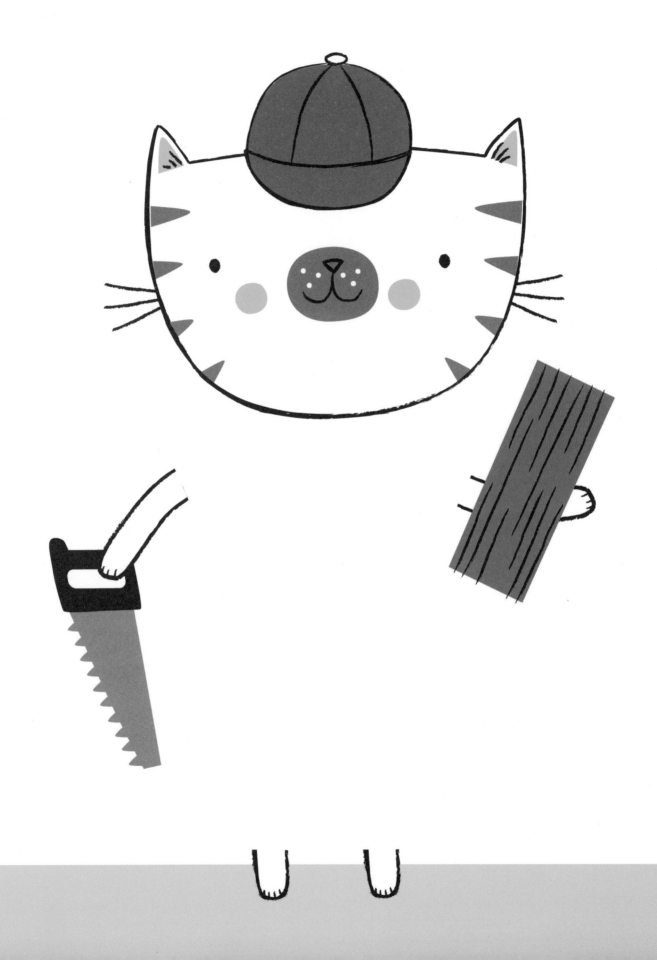

I am a race car driver!

Dress us up as unicorns!

We would like flowery hats, please!

I am a pop star!

I can do handstands!

I like to skateboard!

Dress me up as an alien!

I am a scientist!

We are detectives!

I make cookies!

I'd like a top hat, please!

Dress me up as a mermaid!

I am a fashion designer!

We like making lemonade!

I'm a baker!

We are helicopter pilots!

I like shoes!

Helpful tips!